RACE TO SPACE

BY PATRICIA HUTCHISON

The Child's World®
childsworld.com

Published by The Child's World®
1980 Lookout Drive • Mankato, MN 56003-1705
800-599-READ • www.childsworld.com

Photographs ©: Johnson Space Center/NASA, cover, 1, 5, 6, 9, 20, 25, 26; Fine Art Images Heritage Images/Newscom, 10; Marshall Space Flight Center/NASA, 13, 14; Kennedy Space Center/NASA, 16; Red Line Editorial, 19, 28; Langley Research Center/NASA, 22

Copyright © 2020 by The Child's World®
All rights reserved. No part of this book may be reproduced or utilized in any form or by any means without written permission from the publisher.

ISBN 9781503832206
LCCN 2018962829

Printed in the United States of America
PA02421

ABOUT THE AUTHOR

Patricia Hutchison has written more than a dozen children's books about history and science. She was a teacher for many years. Now she enjoys volunteering as a reading tutor. She also spends time crafting and traveling with her husband.

CONTENTS

FAST FACTS 4

CHAPTER ONE
Heading for the Moon 7

CHAPTER TWO
The Race Begins 11

CHAPTER THREE
So Much to Learn 17

CHAPTER FOUR
Spacecraft Land on the Moon 23

CHAPTER FIVE
Winning the Race 27

Think About It 29
Glossary 30
Source Notes 31
To Learn More 32
Index 32

MOMENTUM

FAST FACTS

Why Was There a Space Race?

▶ After World War II (1939–1945) ended, a new conflict known as the **Cold War** began. The United States and the Soviet Union were competing to advance their technology.

▶ When the Soviet **satellite** *Sputnik 1* launched in 1957, Americans thought the Soviets might use their technology to launch **nuclear weapons** at the United States.

Why Was NASA Started?

▶ Americans were concerned about the Soviet Union's space progress. President Dwight D. Eisenhower established the National Aeronautics and Space Administration (NASA) in 1958. The agency was responsible for coordinating U.S. space exploration.

▶ NASA hired hundreds of women to do calculations for space projects. These women were essential to the space race.

What Effect Did the Space Race Have?

▶ The space race produced powerful technology and weapons, including thousands of nuclear missiles.

The rocket for the Apollo 11 mission launched ▶ from Kennedy Space Center on July 16, 1969.

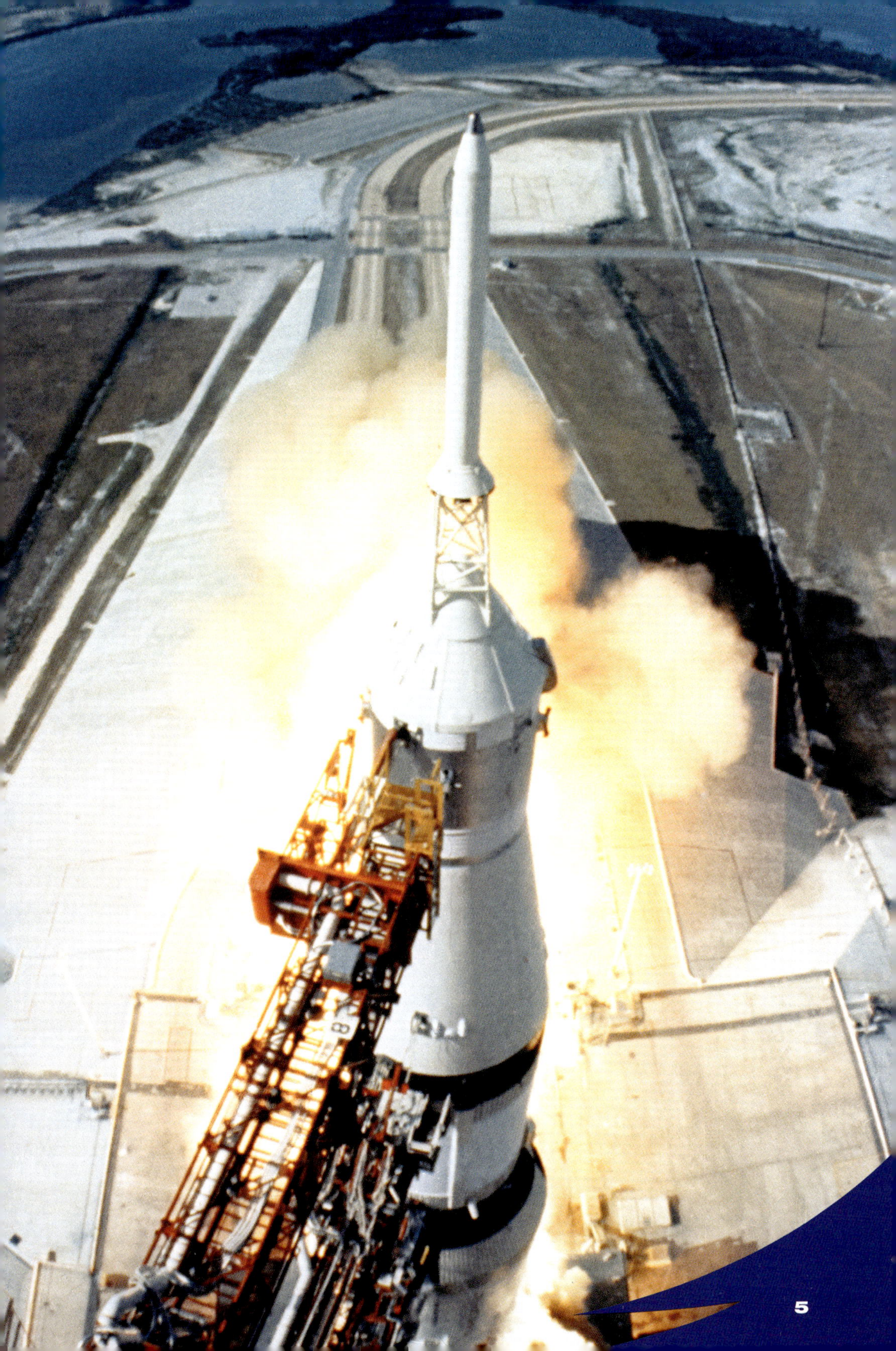

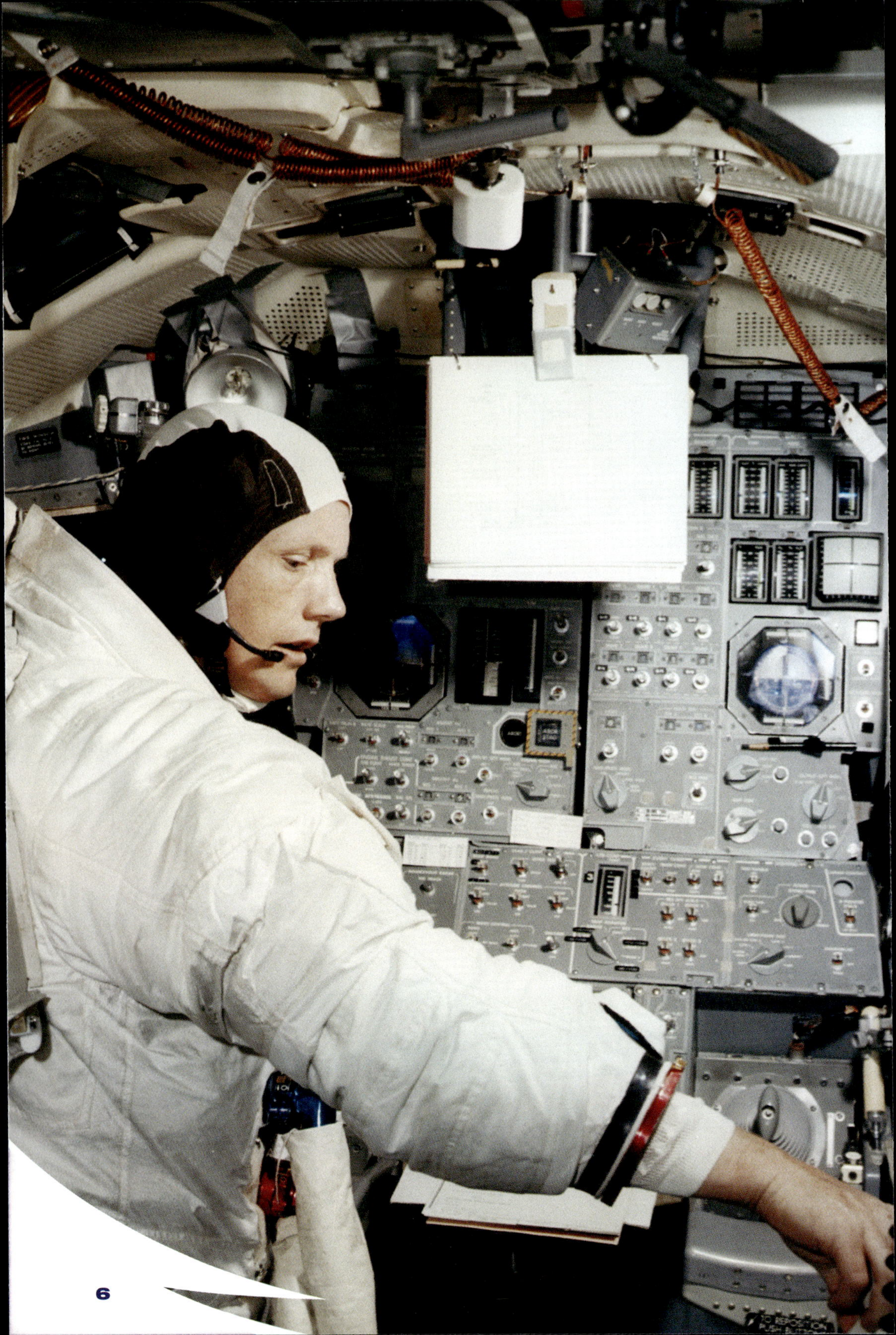

CHAPTER ONE

HEADING FOR THE MOON

The ground trembled, flames shot from the engines, and pillars of smoke rose toward the sky. With a deafening roar, the rocket slowly cleared the launch pad. It was 9:32 a.m. on July 16, 1969. Astronauts Neil Armstrong, Edwin "Buzz" Aldrin, and Michael Collins sat on top of the giant rocket made for the Apollo 11 mission. The men watched Earth shrink as they hurled toward the moon. Americans followed the astronauts' progress, hoping that the mission would end in success. The United States and the Soviet Union were caught up in a fierce contest to see which one would be the first to land a person on the moon.

On July 19, the crew was in **orbit** around the moon. The next day, Armstrong and Aldrin climbed into the **lunar module**, named *Eagle*. Collins stayed alone in the command module, named *Columbia*. The command module would stay in orbit.

◀ Neil Armstrong had to train and prepare for the Apollo 11 mission.

The lunar module would go to the moon's surface. Collins pressed a button and the two spacecraft sprang apart. "The *Eagle* has wings," Armstrong said.[1] The control center in Houston, Texas, gave the go-ahead for *Eagle*'s landing. The astronauts dropped toward the surface. The *Eagle*'s engine fired powerfully.

When the *Eagle* was 50,000 feet (15,240 m) above the surface, a number display blinked a green "99" in the **cockpit**. This meant Armstrong had five seconds to decide to land or go back to the command module. It was now or never. He pressed the button to proceed. The ship dropped 20 feet (6 m) each second. When they were 500 feet (152 m) above the surface, Armstrong looked out and became alarmed. The computer was steering them toward a deep crater the size of a football field. It was dotted with gigantic boulders.

The astronaut knew that *Eagle* would be destroyed if it crashed into the rocks. Thinking quickly, Armstrong took control. He pushed a lever, steering *Eagle* forward. The men sailed over the rocks. Suddenly, alarms began to buzz. *Eagle*'s computer was trying to do too many things at once. Luckily, *Eagle*'s planners had guessed that might happen. The computer dropped the unnecessary tasks and focused on the most important ones. Armstrong continued on, searching for a safe place to land the spacecraft.

▲ **From left to right, Buzz Aldrin, Neil Armstrong, and Michael Collins practiced every moment of their mission before being launched into space.**

Only 60 seconds worth of fuel remained. If *Eagle* ran out of fuel, it would crash into the moon's surface. Armstrong kept going. Thirty seconds of fuel remained. Aldrin looked at the button to **abort** and his heart began to pound.

10

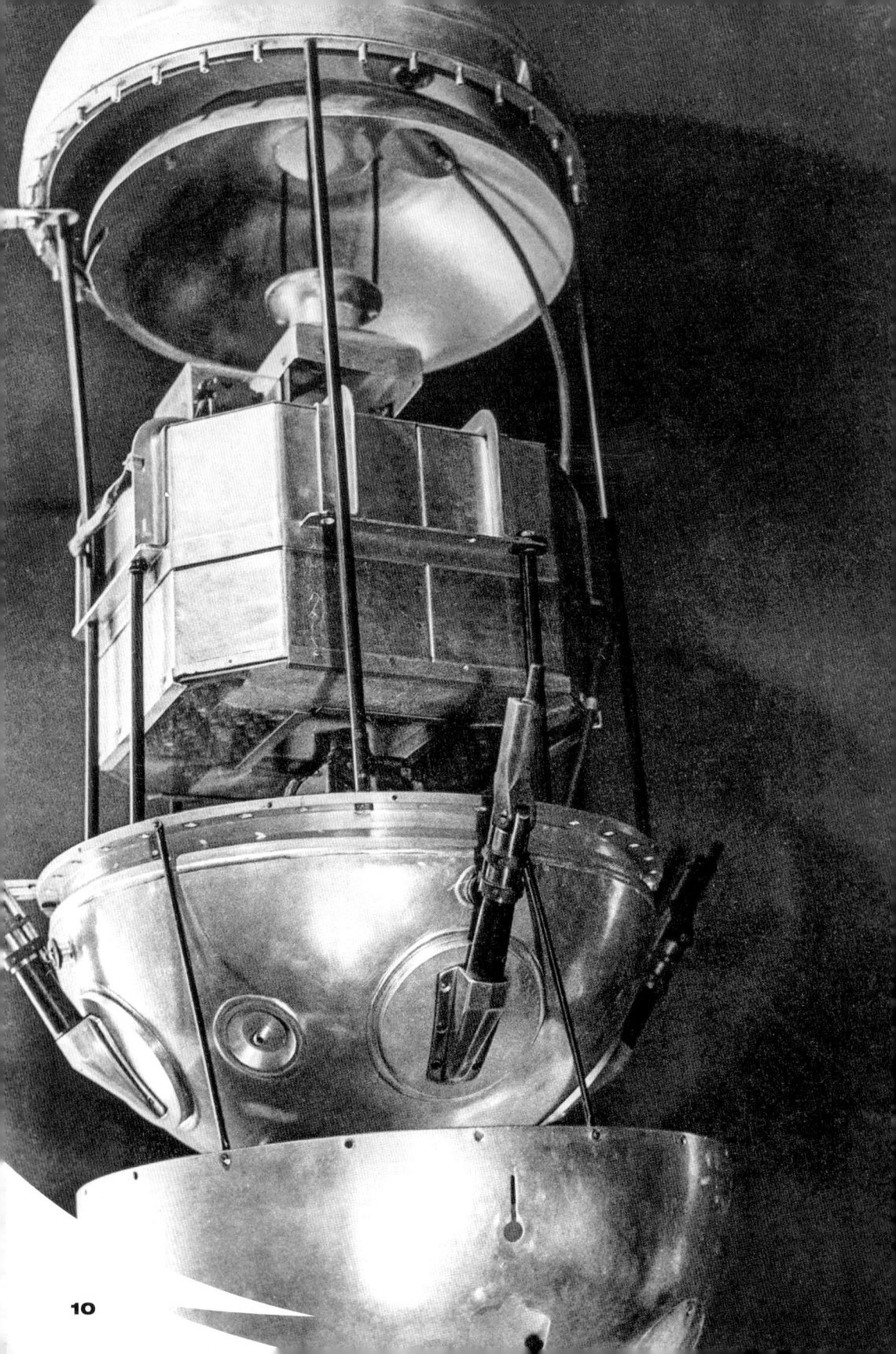

CHAPTER TWO

THE RACE BEGINS

It was October 4, 1957, and many Americans listened to a beeping sound on their radios. The chirping was coming from a beacon in outer space. The Soviet Union had just launched the first man-made object into space. Some Americans could see the satellite dashing across the sky at a speed of 18,000 miles per hour (28,900 kmh). Although it was no bigger than a beach ball, the effect of *Sputnik 1* was huge.

As the satellite orbited Earth, Americans were both shocked and frightened. They were concerned that the Soviets had gotten ahead of the United States in the space race. They also worried that the Soviet accomplishment could give the country a military advantage over the United States. Some people blamed President Dwight D. Eisenhower for letting the United States fall behind. His response was to step up the pace of the U.S. space program.

◄ *Sputnik 1* **had a large battery.**

Two months after *Sputnik 1*'s launch, the United States was ready to show off its own technology. On December 6, 1957, Americans watched eagerly as their new rocket slowly began to rise from the launch pad. In horror, they watched as the rocket sank back down and erupted into a ball of flames.

However, the United States didn't give up. The country launched *Explorer 1* one month later. The satellite, weighing 30 pounds (13.6 kg), was successfully hurled into orbit on January 31, 1958. Six months after that, President Eisenhower authorized the creation of the National Aeronautics and Space Administration (NASA), which would be in charge of the country's space program.

The space race moved quickly. Four months after *Explorer 1* was sent up, the Soviets launched *Sputnik III*. The spacecraft included science equipment. Instruments measured Earth's atmosphere. The Soviets were succeeding in the space race. People wondered if the United States would be able to keep up.

President John F. Kennedy, who entered office in 1961, believed the United States could not only keep up, but also race ahead. On May 25, 1961, he addressed Congress. The president's goal was to send a man to the moon and return him safely to Earth. He challenged NASA to do this before the decade ended.

A launch team worked in the control ▶ room during *Explorer 1*'s liftoff.

13

14

NASA had a lot of work to do. The first step would be to send a human off the planet.

But the Soviets had already beaten the Americans to it. Soviet **cosmonaut** Yuri Gagarin lifted off in *Vostok 1* on April 12, 1961. He flew 108 minutes, making one orbit around Earth. When he was over Africa, *Vostok 1*'s engines fired to bring him back. When Gagarin returned to Moscow, the capital of the Soviet Union, thousands of people greeted him as a hero.

Astronaut Alan Shepard was frustrated that the United States did not win this important part of the race. But NASA was being cautious. The U.S. mission to launch a man into space was delayed many times for tests. At last, on May 5, 1961, Shepard got his chance. That day, agonizing delays pushed the launch time back more than two hours. Finally, at 9:34 a.m., the rocket rumbled into space. Shepard flew 116 miles (186 km) above Earth. His mission was not to orbit Earth, but to fly into space and come back safely. When he came back to Earth, Shepard splashed down in the Atlantic Ocean and was picked up by the U.S. Navy.

◄ **Alan Shepard was launched in the *Freedom 7* spacecraft.**

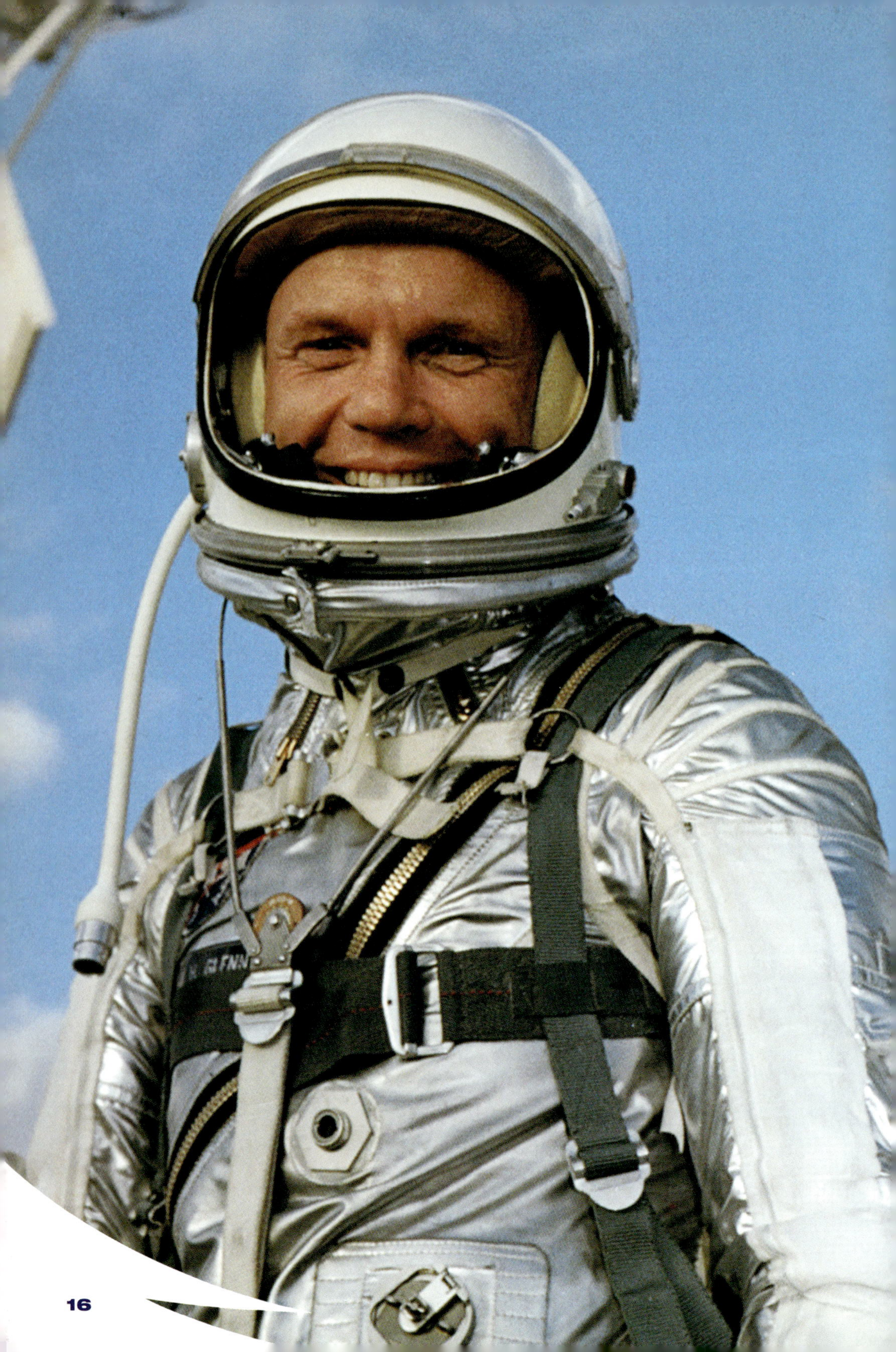

CHAPTER THREE

SO MUCH TO LEARN

John Glenn flew up and down in a plane nicknamed the Vomit Comet. He was training to be an astronaut for NASA. As if on a roller coaster ride, he and the other trainees felt as if they were weightless at the top of the hill. Some of them felt sick, but Glenn didn't. He walked on the ceiling and did flips in the air. He also completed other tests with great success.

His three years of training paid off. On February 20, 1962, Glenn climbed into the tiny cone of the *Friendship 7* spacecraft and launched into space. Hours later, during his third orbit around Earth, he looked down at the United States. He was 162 miles (260 km) above the ground and could see the whole state of Florida. Glenn was the first American to orbit Earth, reaching speeds of 17,000 miles per hour (27,300 kmh). After coming down to Earth, he became an instant hero.

◀ **John Glenn spent four hours and 55 minutes in flight in the *Friendship 7* spacecraft.**

Glenn's success inspired the United States. But there was a lot to learn before NASA spacecraft could land on the moon. Many questions had to be answered. Could humans survive many days in space? Could they stay alive outside the rocket, wearing only a spacesuit? Could they connect two spacecraft in orbit after one blasted off the moon? A successful moon mission would require all these things. To find answers, NASA started the Gemini program.

Launched in June 1965, Gemini IV was NASA's second manned space flight. While in orbit, astronaut Edward White got ready to take a walk in space. He was excited for the mission. He pulled the handle to open the hatch on the spacecraft. He floated outside the capsule, attached by a **tether** that pumped oxygen to his spacesuit.

But White was not the first person to walk in space. The Soviets also had beaten the Americans to that milestone. In March 1965, cosmonaut Alexei Leonov exited his rocket. He was the first human to see Earth from the outside of a spacecraft. But the mission did not go well. Leonov's spacesuit expanded like a balloon. He had to work so hard to get back into the craft that sweat coated his body. At the end of the flight, the rocket landed hundreds of miles away from its intended target and in feet of snow.

WHAT SHOULD NASA FOCUS ON TODAY?

NASA has done many different types of space missions. In 2018, people had different opinions on what NASA should focus on.

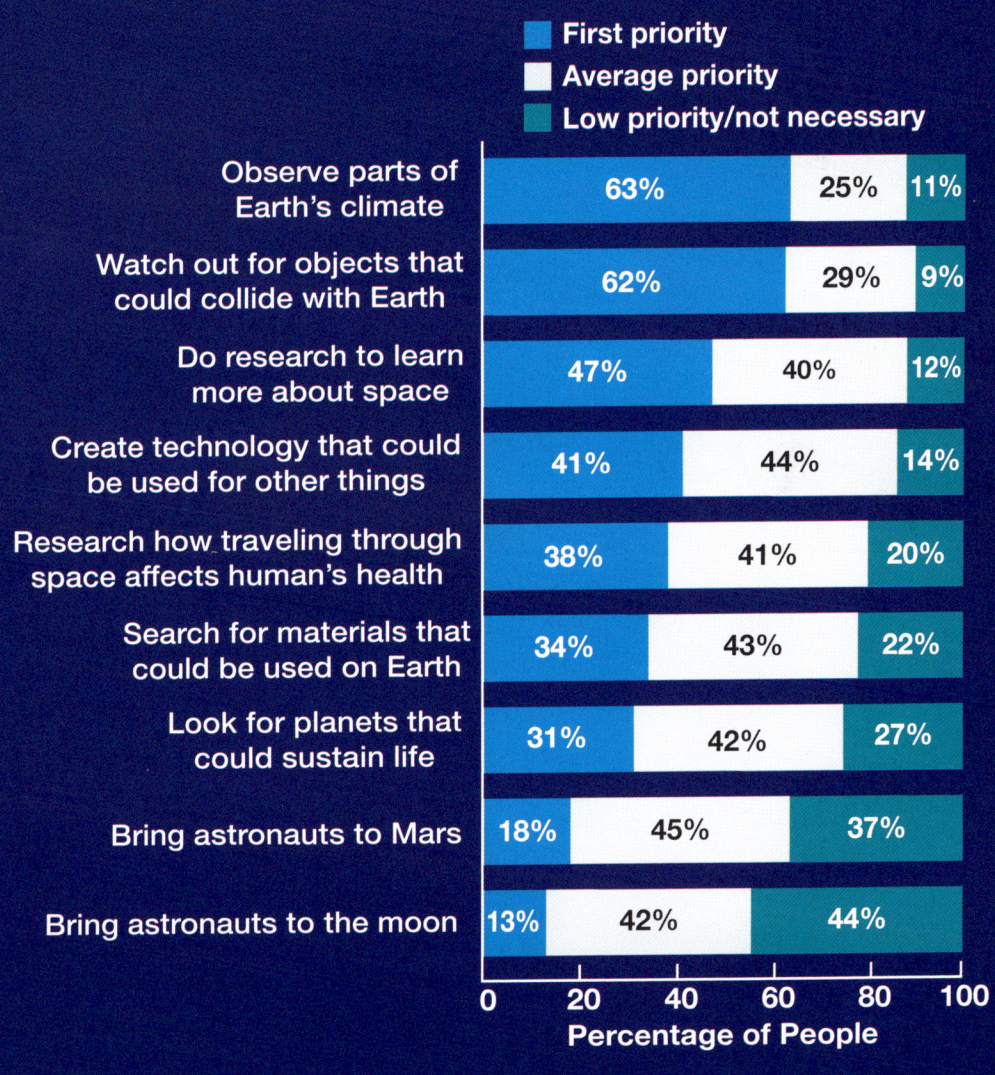

Legend:
- First priority
- Average priority
- Low priority/not necessary

Focus Area	First priority	Average priority	Low priority/not necessary
Observe parts of Earth's climate	63%	25%	11%
Watch out for objects that could collide with Earth	62%	29%	9%
Do research to learn more about space	47%	40%	12%
Create technology that could be used for other things	41%	44%	14%
Research how traveling through space affects human's health	38%	41%	20%
Search for materials that could be used on Earth	34%	43%	22%
Look for planets that could sustain life	31%	42%	27%
Bring astronauts to Mars	18%	45%	37%
Bring astronauts to the moon	13%	42%	44%

Percentage of People

Numbers do not always equal 100% because of rounding

▲ **Edward White drifted in space for about 20 minutes before going back inside the spacecraft.**

Meanwhile, the Soviet Union had tried twice to connect spacecraft in orbit. But the missions failed. In December 1965, NASA's *Gemini VI* and *VII* were able to maintain a distance of 1 foot (0.3 m) apart. So far, this was the closest any two rockets had flown together in orbit. The United States shot into the lead in the space race.

In March 1966, another Gemini mission took place to connect two spacecraft in orbit. A radio-controlled target vehicle launched first. Then, astronauts Armstrong and David Scott left the launch pad in *Gemini VIII*. After four hours, the astronauts caught up with the target. Soon, Scott radioed Mission Control, reporting that the two spacecraft docked smoothly. The United States had taken a giant step toward the moon.

TAKING A WILD RIDE

After *Gemini VIII* docked with its target, everyone breathed a sigh of relief. Then, Scott radioed that there was a serious problem. The connected spacecraft were beginning to spin wildly. Armstrong made a decision. He shut down the thrusters. Then, he separated from the target spacecraft. But the spinning continued. Finally, Armstrong brought the spinning under control. But now they were running out of fuel. Mission Control guided them in an emergency landing. The men splashed down safely but bobbed in the ocean for three hours, waiting to be picked up by the U.S. Navy. They were seasick but unharmed.

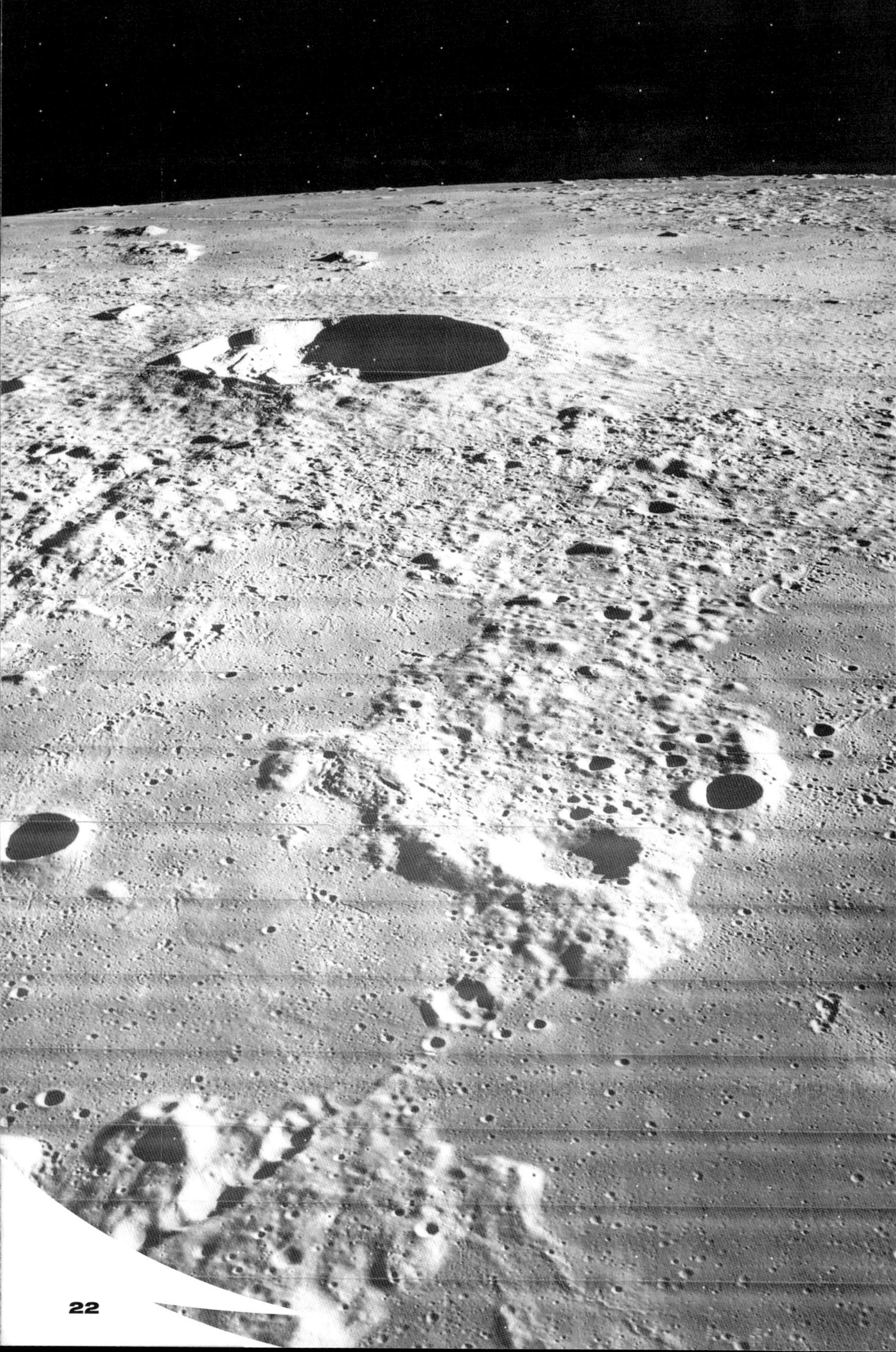

CHAPTER FOUR

SPACECRAFT LAND ON THE MOON

The Soviets' unmanned *Luna 9* spacecraft approached the moon on February 3, 1966. Just before landing, a 5-foot (1.5 m) capsule shot out of the rocket. It bounced several times on the surface and then stopped. Its television system began sending pictures back to Earth. The first images were very blurry. But as the sun rose, they became clearer. The pictures showed wide views of the moon's surface. The Soviets were proud of being the first to land a spacecraft on the moon.

Almost six months later, scientists in California were controlling the first U.S. lunar lander, called *Surveyor 1*. The craft settled softly on the moon's surface. Soon, it began sending amazing photos of the moon to Earth.

◄ **Photos of the moon's surface showed people that it had many craters.**

Scientists were thrilled. *Surveyor 1*'s success put the American goal of landing men on the moon about one year ahead of schedule. It was time for NASA to begin its Apollo program.

On January 27, 1967, astronauts Edward White, Gus Grissom, and Roger Chaffee sat in the command module for the Apollo 1 mission. They were about to practice for their upcoming flight. At 6:31 p.m., Mission Control heard a scream. One of the men cried out, "We have a fire in the cockpit!"[2] The command module burst and flames shot out. The crew died in seconds. The disaster shocked the nation. The tragedy delayed the Apollo program for 18 months.

After the Apollo 1 failure, the Soviets hoped they could beat the United States to the moon. On April 24, 1967, cosmonaut Vladimir Komarov blasted off in *Soyuz 1*. Three other cosmonauts were set to launch in *Soyuz 2* and dock in space. The Soviet Union was excited about its first manned mission in more than two years. But their joy turned quickly to heartbreak. One of *Soyuz 1*'s solar panels failed. It was only receiving one-half the power it needed. The Soviets tried to bring Komarov back safely, but the rocket's parachutes also failed. The capsule hit the ground and burst into flames. Komarov died instantly.

From left to right, Gus Grissom, Roger Chaffee, and Edward White checked out the command module while in their space suits.

25

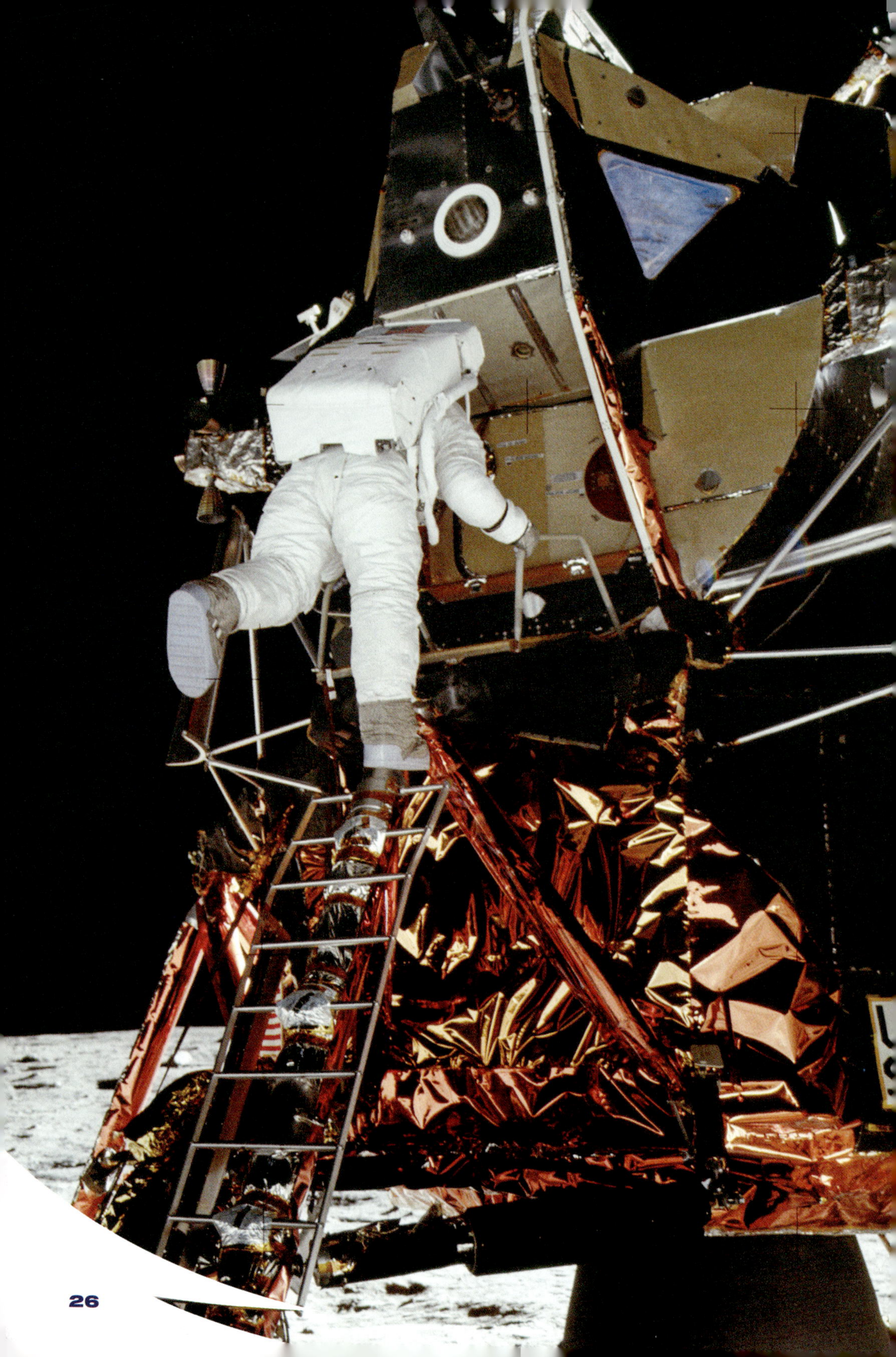

CHAPTER FIVE

WINNING THE RACE

On July 20, 1969, Armstrong was looking for a safe place to land *Eagle*. Fuel was running low. He maneuvered the craft away from the large crater and settled it on the moon with a slight jolt. Calmly, Armstrong radioed to Mission Control: "The *Eagle* has landed."[3] Hours later, Armstrong opened *Eagle*'s hatch. He stepped slowly down the ladder to a place where no one had ever walked before. As he planted his foot on the surface of the moon, he declared, "That's one small step for a man, one giant leap for mankind."[4] Cameras attached to the outside the craft **broadcast** the astronaut's movements. Millions of people on Earth watched in awe.

Later, Aldrin joined Armstrong on the surface. Together, they scooped up soil and rock samples. After doing a few scientific experiments, the men planted a U.S. flag into the ground.

◀ **Armstrong photographed Aldrin as he exited *Eagle* and prepared to walk on the moon.**

TIMELINE OF THE RACE TO SPACE

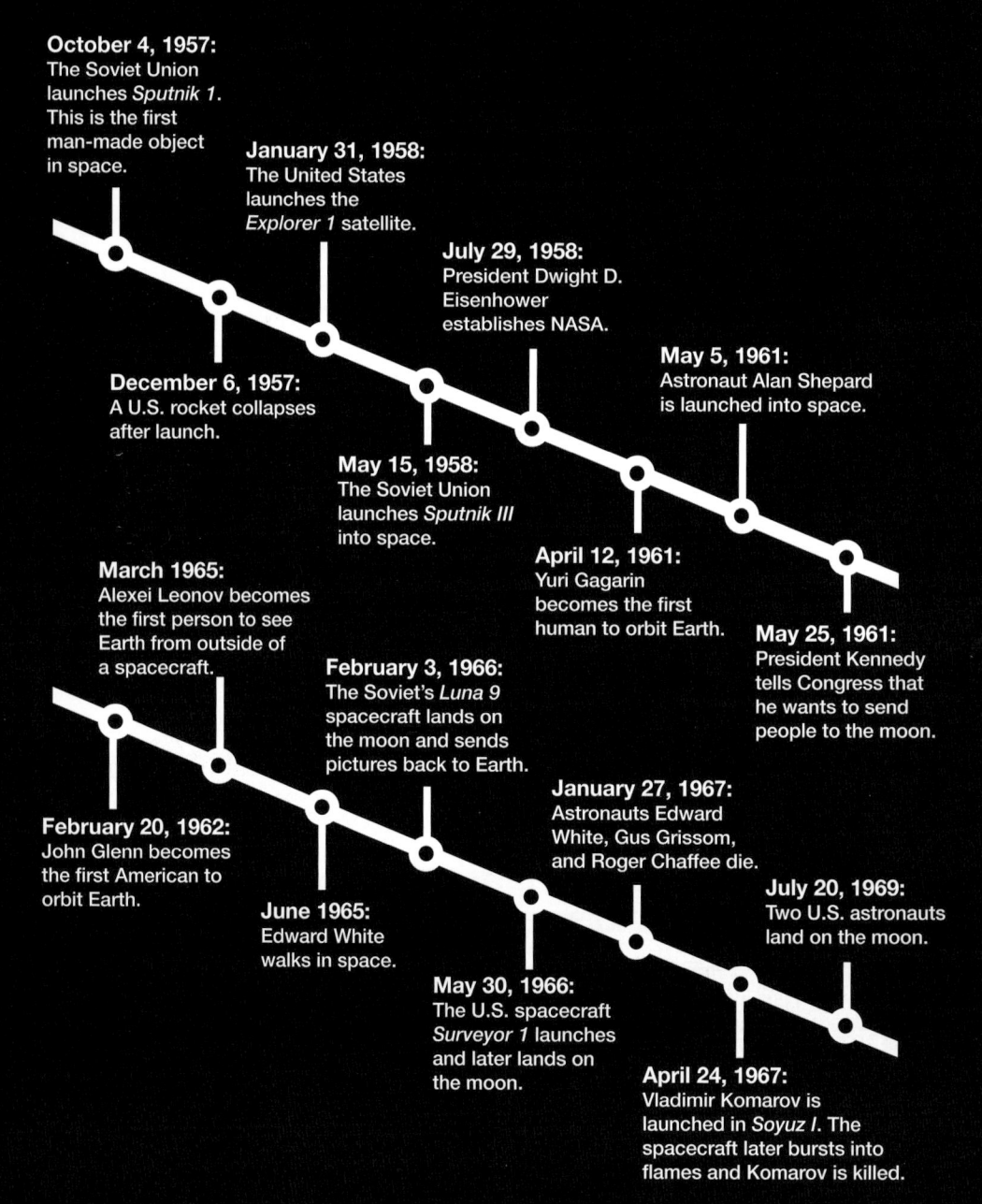

October 4, 1957: The Soviet Union launches *Sputnik 1*. This is the first man-made object in space.

December 6, 1957: A U.S. rocket collapses after launch.

January 31, 1958: The United States launches the *Explorer 1* satellite.

May 15, 1958: The Soviet Union launches *Sputnik III* into space.

July 29, 1958: President Dwight D. Eisenhower establishes NASA.

April 12, 1961: Yuri Gagarin becomes the first human to orbit Earth.

May 5, 1961: Astronaut Alan Shepard is launched into space.

May 25, 1961: President Kennedy tells Congress that he wants to send people to the moon.

February 20, 1962: John Glenn becomes the first American to orbit Earth.

March 1965: Alexei Leonov becomes the first person to see Earth from outside of a spacecraft.

June 1965: Edward White walks in space.

February 3, 1966: The Soviet's *Luna 9* spacecraft lands on the moon and sends pictures back to Earth.

May 30, 1966: The U.S. spacecraft *Surveyor 1* launches and later lands on the moon.

January 27, 1967: Astronauts Edward White, Gus Grissom, and Roger Chaffee die.

April 24, 1967: Vladimir Komarov is launched in *Soyuz I*. The spacecraft later bursts into flames and Komarov is killed.

July 20, 1969: Two U.S. astronauts land on the moon.

When their work was done, they took some time to have a little fun. Hopping and leaping around, they demonstrated what it was like to move about in reduced gravity.

Soon, it was time to return to *Eagle*. They blasted off the moon and reconnected with the command module. Then, they headed for Earth. The United States had won the race to the moon.

Throughout the 2000s, the United States, Russia, and several other countries worked together on the International Space Station. Flying 248 miles (399 km) above Earth, scientists perform experiments both inside and outside the craft. Their main mission is to figure out how to protect the human body during space missions to other planets. Where will humans go next?

THINK ABOUT IT

- Why do you think so many people are interested in space missions?
- If you had the chance, would you take part in a space mission? Why or why not?
- Do you think the space race was helpful or harmful for the two countries and the world? Give reasons for your answer.

GLOSSARY

abort (uh-BORT): To abort means to stop something early on because of an issue. Aldrin wondered if he should abort the mission.

broadcast (BRAWD-kast): Events that are broadcast are made public over television or radio. The moon landing was broadcast all over the world.

cockpit (KAHK-pit): The cockpit is an area in a spacecraft where the pilot and crew sit. The astronaut climbed into the small cockpit.

Cold War (KOHLD WOR): The Cold War was when the United States and the Soviet Union were politically hostile toward one another. The Cold War lasted from 1947 to 1991.

cosmonaut (KOZ-muh-nawt): A cosmonaut is a Russian or Soviet space explorer. Yuri Gagarin was a Soviet cosmonaut.

lunar module (LOO-nur MOJ-ool): A lunar module is a space vehicle used to transport astronauts to the moon from the command module. Armstrong and Aldrin were in the lunar module *Eagle*.

nuclear weapons (NOO-klee-ur WEP-uhns): Nuclear weapons are powerful weapons that use energy from splitting atoms. The United States worried that the Soviet Union would use nuclear weapons.

orbit (OR-bit): Orbit is the path followed by a planet, moon, or other object as it goes around a planet, moon, or the sun. Astronauts went into orbit around the moon.

satellite (SAT-uh-lite): A satellite is a man-made object that orbits bodies such as the moon or Earth. *Sputnik I* was the first satellite in space.

tether (TETH-ur): A tether is a line that fastens something to another object so that it can only move a limited distance. The astronaut's tether kept him from floating off into space.

SOURCE NOTES

1. Bob Granath. "Neil Armstrong Praised as a Reluctant American Hero." *NASA*. National Aeronautics and Space Administration, 30 Aug. 2012. Web. 3 Jan. 2019.

2. Sarah Larimer. "'We Have a Fire in the Cockpit!' The Apollo 1 Disaster 50 Years Later." *Washington Post*. Washington Post, 26 Jan. 2017. Web. 3 Jan. 2019.

3. "Wide Awake on the Sea of Tranquility." *NASA*. National Aeronautics and Space Administration, 9 July 2014. Web. 3 Jan. 2019.

4. "July 20, 1969: One Giant Leap for Mankind." *NASA*. National Aeronautics and Space Administration, 20 July 2017. Web. 3 Jan. 2019.

TO LEARN MORE

BOOKS

Adamson, Thomas K. *Apollo 11 Launches a New Era.* Mankato, MN: The Child's World, 2019.

Aldrin, Buzz. *To the Moon and Back.* Washington, DC: National Geographic Kids, 2018.

Zoehfeld, Kathleen Weidner. *Apollo 13: How Three Brave Astronauts Survived a Space Disaster.* New York, NY: Random House, 2015.

WEBSITES

Visit our website for links about the race to space:
childsworld.com/links

Note to Parents, Teachers, and Librarians: We routinely verify our Web links to make sure they are safe and active sites. So encourage your readers to check them out!

INDEX

Aldrin, Edwin "Buzz," 7–9, 27, 29
Armstrong, Neil, 7–9, 21, 27, 29

Chaffee, Roger, 24
Collins, Michael, 7–8

Eisenhower, Dwight D., 4, 11–12
Explorer 1, 12

Gagarin, Yuri, 15
Glenn, John, 17–18
Grissom, Gus, 24

International Space Station, 29

Kennedy, John F., 12

Mission Control, 21, 24, 27

National Aeronautics and Space Administration (NASA), 4, 12, 15, 17–18, 20, 24

Shepard, Alan, 15
Sputnik 1, 4, 11–12
Surveyor 1, 23–24

White, Edward, 18, 24

32